The Peak District
Its Secrets & Curiosities

*Dedicated to my children: Amanda,
Rebecca, Andrew, Alistair and Phillip*

THE
PEAK DISTRICT

ITS SECRETS *&* CURIOSITIES

Lindsey Porter

MPC

British Library Cataloguing in
Publication Data:
Porter, Lindsey
  The Peak District : its secrets and
  curiosities
  1. England. Peak District - Visitor's
  guides
  I. Title
  914.25'1104858

Cover Photograph:
Abandoned millstones near Bole Hill
Quarry near Hathersage (MPC picture
collection)

The photograph on page 98 was supplied by the Peak District Mining
Museum, Matlock Bath; all other photographs are from the MPC Picture
Collection.

Published by:
Moorland Publishing Co Ltd,
Moor Farm Road,
Ashbourne,
Derbyshire DE6 1HD
England

ISBN 0 86190 240 8

Printed in the UK by:
Billings, Worcester

Contents

Introduction

In 1977 I was approached by Frank Rodgers who asked me to consider publishing his manuscript, which appeared the following year as *Curiosities of the Peak District*. The book was well received but I felt that there was still a need to produce a book which took an in depth look at some of the more unusual aspects of the Peak.

Many of the features selected are not necessarily unusual in a wider context. For instance the country is well endowed with medieval wayside crosses, but the quantity in the Peak is more restricted. Surviving riverside mills powered by waterwheels are common elsewhere but there is not one example open to the public within the National Park, which retains its wheels despite several mills which slumber on with some or all of their machinery largely intact.

The purpose of this book therefore, is to highlight features which are often missed, even in the most visited areas and to encourage the exploration of places away from the main tourist areas. One has only to think of the thousands who swarm up to Dovedale and wonder how many of them realise the dale is one of the last survivors of a relict ash wood in the country; how many of them look for Beresford Tower or the Watch Box and how many know that the upper Dove Valley has much to offer the discerning visitor who prefers a greater degree of solitude?

The selection of items to include is subjective. I have tried to avoid repeating items Frank Rodgers selected for his book although I felt a few items needed including for completeness, especially as my approach has been a thematic one. One can hardly say that many people miss places like Thor's Cave in the Manifold Valley, but I felt it should be included. None the less, I have excluded a few interesting items which are off the beaten track in an endeavour to discourage trespass and damage, unless a feature can be seen from the road or path. A good example is the chambered tomb of Five Wells, which is excluded. Included are Charles Cotton's Fishing House and Beresford Tower which are visible from the valley path in Beresford Dale. Wilful trespass cannot be condoned under any circumstances and this book encourages exploration with this in mind.

This is my fifth book on the Peak District as a whole. My editorial colleagues at Moorland Publishing and a few reviewers persist in the view that I continually include a few items which cannot be construed as being within the Peak District. They are, of course, strictly accurate. The Churnet Valley is not in the Peak District *per se*. However, I remain convinced that visitors to the area want to obtain the best from their holiday or visit. They are as inquisitive as I am and I stick to my policy firmly in the belief that if my digressions bring a bit more pleasure then all is worthwhile.

Finally, I have to acknowledge the use I have made of the Derbyshire and Staffordshire volumes of Pevsner's *Buildings of England* series, plus *Peakland Roads and Trackways* by A.E. & E.M. Dodd. Although the latter is now out of print, I recommend this book to all with a love of Peakland history. I should also like to thank Mary Winstone of Clifton, Ashbourne for allowing me to use her photograph of Penelope Boothby's tomb and The Chatsworth House Trust for the photograph of the Chatsworth chapel.

C.L.M. Porter

Natural Features

Limestone's propensity to dissolve results in many unusual features in the landscape. Cave systems abound, and rock pillars are common, although not often as tall as the Dovedale examples. In the Manifold Valley lies one of the largest underground river systems in the Peak — perhaps the largest. The river disappears at Wetton Mill and bubbles up again at Ilam in the 'boil holes' in the grounds of the Hall, some 22 hours later. The River Hamps does likewise at Waterhouses and reappears a few feet from the Manifold at Ilam. The Manifold Valley also has a relic of a former underground river system, now left high and dry some 250ft above the river and known as Thor's Cave.

Around the turn of the century, Sir Thomas Wardle, who lived at Swainsley Hall in the Manifold Valley, tried to prevent the water flowing underground. Areas of the river bed known to contain swallet holes were lined with concrete. However, the air pressure created when water started to flow underground through other unsealed holes caused the concrete to crack. In an effort to combat this, ventilation pipes were sunk into the river bed — possibly into swallet holes. The theory being that the trapped air could escape up the pipes. This too was unsuccessful and slabs of concrete and the ventilation pipes remain to this day.

1   Thor's Cave

2-3 Here are the boil holes (left) at Ilam and a couple of ventilation pipes (below) approximately a half-mile above Weag's Bridge.

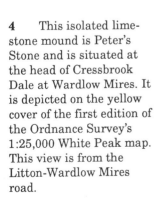

4   This isolated lime-stone mound is Peter's Stone and is situated at the head of Cressbrook Dale at Wardlow Mires. It is depicted on the yellow cover of the first edition of the Ordnance Survey's 1:25,000 White Peak map. This view is from the Litton-Wardlow Mires road.

Dovedale justifies its reputation, held now for centuries, concerning its spectacular beauty. The growth of sycamore and the volume of visitors has done nothing to sustain the beauty. Fortunately, this has been recognised by the National Trust who have removed many of the intruding trees and scrub to reveal the rock faces. There has been much misplaced criticism in this respect, but the dale now has a much greater resemblance to the Dovedale that our Victorian ancestors knew.

The dale contains perhaps the tallest free-standing pillars in the Peak (unless one includes The Tower at Alport Castles as a pillar). Here is a trio of Victorian views of the dale showing features well known to visitors in those days. It is fascinating to compare the views today; the footpath was clearly well-trodden but not the intrusive causeway of today. On the right of Pickering Tor is a huge cube of rock known as 'The Watchbox'. It had a reputation for being capable of being rocked, but it is little known today.

REYNARD'S CAVE, DOVE DALE   3924   G.W.W.

5   Reynard's Arch

6 Ilam Rock

8   The gritstone escarpment of the Roaches in the south-west of the Peak offers some of the best walking in the district, especially if one encompasses the valleys which cut deep into Axe Edge to the north of the Roaches. The eastern escarpment fronts the road from Leek to Buxton and is known as Ramshaw Rocks. One clearly noticeable rock (above, right) juts out towards the road and looks like a face. There is even a hole for the eye and as you draw level with it (driving towards Buxton) it 'winks' at you!

9   A more significant natural feature than the 'Winking Eye' lies to the west of Gradbach below the westward extension of the outcrop which runs from the Roaches to Danebridge. Here, at Lud Church, a landslip has created a huge crevasse. It is at least 60ft high and 200ft long. This view shows a wooden statue of Lady Lud which stood at the northern end for many years. Access to Lud Church is best achieved from Castor's Bridge across the Black Brook at its confluence with the River Dane.

10   A further landslip has produced this isolated mass of rock. The rock, known as The Tower, has moved away from Alport Castles, the name of the rock face nearby. It lies to the east of Alport Castles Farm which lies at the head of the Alport Dale. This quiet valley cuts a decisive slice out of the desolate Bleaklow moors. It can be reached by parking at Alport Bridge, west of Ladybower Reservoir on the Snake Road, and walking up the valley on the north side of the road.

11   South of Bleaklow is Kinder Scout and on its western flank, above Hayfield is Kinder Down-fall, a distinctive waterfall, perhaps the highest in the Peak. It is well known for blowing back in high wind and even freezing up altogether in winter.

12   On the eastern gritstone edge near The Fox House Inn is this delightful rock known as The Toad's Mouth Rock. Only the eye is artificial.

13   At the bottom of the Winnats Pass is the Speedwell Cavern. This is an old lead mine which used boats on an underground canal. Visitors are taken along the old mine level in a boat in the same way as the old miners. The mine had a short history. It started in 1771 and £14,000 was expended to produce lead ore to a value of less than £3,000. It closed in 1790. At the far end of the mine is a huge cave system known as the 'Bottomless Pit', which was welcomed by the miners who poured their waste water and stone into it.

14   The Winnats Pass cuts a deep slice out of the limestone plateau to the north-west of Castleton. It is thought to have been formed under the sea from currents eroding the seabed. It has been used as a road for centuries and for a long time was disfigured by telegraph poles. Since the abandonment due to slippage of the road under Mam Tor, which was built in 1811 to avoid the steep gradients of the Winnats Pass, the original turnpike road up the Winnats Pass is again the only direct route to Castleton from the west.

15 West of Castleton are two large cave systems. Eldon Hole (pictured) lies on the south side of Eldon Hill, better known for its huge quarry. The chasm has a drop of 180ft. To the north is Giant's Hole which was found to connect to Oxlow Caverns in 1966. The combined system now gives cavers over 3 miles of passages and the second deepest cave in the British Isles. Eldon Hole may be viewed from a path that runs eastwards from the end of Eldon Lane, near Peak Forest village. The hole may be seen on the side of the hill north of the path.

16 This photograph is taken on the peat-covered Kinder Scout plateau, just north of Eldon Hole. The rainwater runs off in little rivulets which have created a deeply incised drainage pattern across the plateau. The rivulets frequently open right down to the underlying bed-rock. The remaining peat areas are known as 'hags' and the miniature valleys as 'groughs'. Occasionally remains of tree roots can be found and — if you are lucky — flint microliths of prehistoric man who used them to create barbs on arrows etc.

Home and Village Life

Changes in domestic life have been dramatic both in urban and rural communities. Perhaps in the latter, more examples of days gone by survive, such as pinfolds, village wells, market halls, dovecotes etc.

Here is a collection of interesting houses and features connected with domestic life across the Peak, from the tragic graves of plague victims to ornate village wells and pretty village schools.

17   Today the buildings across the Peak are traditionally roofed with tiles (chiefly Staffordshire Blue), gritstone shingles (thin layers of stone) or slate. However many houses were roofed with thatch. Today very few examples survive in the area. Among them is this example by the Bar Brook at Nether End, Baslow. There is another east of Wirksworth on Wirksworth moor, several in Osmaston village near Ashbourne and of course the delightfully re-roofed cottages north of Pilsley on the Chatsworth to Baslow road.

18 Now known as the Old House Museum in Bakewell, this house (above) was built in 1543. It has been restored and now displays its original wattle and daub interior walls. It was extended in about 1620 and converted into tenements by Sir Richard Arkwright in about 1790.

19-20 Edensor village (below and opposite) was re-built out of the sight of Chatsworth by the sixth Duke of Devonshire, between 1838-42. Apparently, the Duke couldn't decide which style to build and chose one of each design. The village is a fascinating collection of different styles.

21   This is Riber Castle, built between 1862-8 by John Smedley as his residence. Smedley owned the huge hydro which now houses the County Offices in Matlock. The castle dominates the skyline from Matlock and its publicity value could not have been lost on him.

22   A contrast is the Old Hall at Fenny Bentley which still retains its medieval tower, visible from the A515. The tower is the remnant of a fortified house that occupied a moated site. It was owned by the Beresford family and passed by marriage into the estate of Charles Cotton. An unusual memorial of 1473 to the Beresfords exists in Fenny Bentley church. It was carved without knowledge of the facial features of the deceased and therefore shows Thomas Beresford and his wife Elizabeth completely wrapped in a shroud, tied above the head. Their children appear on the side of the tomb in a similar manner.

23 Gawsworth Hall is situated just to the south of Macclesfield in Cheshire. It is a beautiful building with a large expanse of lawn sloping down to an equally large lake. The oldest part of the house is on the southerly side and dates from 1480. Much of the original building was demolished in 1701, when it was in very poor repair. This building extended towards the tilting ground where knights jousted until the end of the sixteenth century. The tilting ground may still be seen, a rare survivor of a bygone age.

24 Hartington Hall is sometimes described as the best surviving example in the Peak of a Derbyshire yeoman's house and farm. It is also the oldest surviving youth hostel in the Peak, having opened in 1934, just ahead of Ilam Hall. It was the home of the Bateman family who kept it until about 35 years ago, maintaining a small suite of rooms. The oldest part, the south elevation, dates from 1611. The remaining parts followed in 1861, 2 years after the large range of farm buildings. Finally, the double bay on the west front was added in 1911, 300 years after the south front was built.

25   Lea Rhododendron Garden was originally established as a quiet retreat by John Marsden Smedley of the adjacent seat of Lea Green. He planted many different species of rhododendron over 20 years or so in an old quarry. Today the site has matured and is carefully tended by its owner. Over 500 varieties of rhododendron may be seen. In spring, this garden is a mass of colour with many varieties in flower and is well worth a visit.

The market hall was often a focal point of village life in those places lucky enough to have a charter to hold a market. Here are pictured three examples which survive within the upland area of the Peak, rather than in towns which surround it.

26   Although detail relating to a charter at Longnor is obscure, this village was an important market town, on a par with nearby Leek at one time. The market hall is dated 1873. The plaque lists a 'Table of Tolls payable at Longnor Markets and Fairs'. The prices are for buyers and sellers.

27 Winster's market hall dates from either the fifteenth or sixteenth century. The first floor is later. This building was the first property to be acquired in Derbyshire by the National Trust. The side arches have been infilled to strengthen the structure.

28 The market hall at Bakewell was built in the early part of the seventeenth century, it is now a Peak District National Park Information Centre.

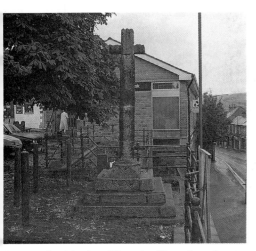

29   The Market Place in Chapel-en-le-Frith where the market cross and stocks survive.

30   This is the Butter Cross at Leek (right). It was erected by the Joliffe family in 1671 and originally occupied the site at the junction of Sheep Market and Stanley Street at the bottom of the Market Place. It was removed in 1806 and ended up in the cemetery in 1857. It was restored to the Market Place in 1986. It would have been the focal point of much activity on market days.

31   Village schools are being phased out as a result of consolidation on fewer sites. A delightfully designed village school is this one in Ilam, built in 1854, when the whole village was part of the Ilam estate of the Watts-Russell family. To the rear, on the left-hand side is the school master's house.

32   Hollinsclough school, now replaced by a modern and more functional building at the rear.

If animals strayed onto the highway, they were rounded up and impounded in the village pinfold until the owner could be located.

33   Biggin Pinfold

34   Curbar (left) opposite the aptly named Pinfold Hill

35   Hathersage Pinfold, situated in Church Lane

The horse was an essential part of everyday life and troughs of water supplied water for the horse as well as domestic life. The well or spring was therefore an integral part of the village. Well dressing is a popular pastime in many Peak District villages although many wells are now covered over. Wirksworth for example has a well dressing ceremony, although no wells can be seen today! Here are a few of the more unusual troughs.

36 Eyam village — part of the 1588 village water supply system, one of the oldest village systems in the county.

37 Near Gradbach Mill, with a seat each side.

38 Wildboarclough — a collection of troughs arranged in a semi-circle at Crag Hall.

39 Hall Well, Tissington — a rather weathered stone says 'Restored 1860 [?] J. Hardy'.

40 Curbar Well, at the top of Pinfold Hill (where there is this unusual covered well and the round trough). The other stones are millstones sunk into the ground.

41 High Well, Taddington

42   Wildboarclough used to be quite an industrial place with a large complex of mill buildings. The mill manager's house survives along with the office block. The latter is now an attractive dwelling house but used to be Wildboarclough Post Office. In fact it was supposedly the largest sub post office in the country!

43   One of the oldest post boxes in the country is in Buxton, opposite the entrance to the Opera House. It still displays the monogram 'VR'.

There are many pitiful reminders of the plague. Bodies were often interred away from the community and there must be many that still lie unmarked, hastily buried to prevent the spread of infection. Some are marked, such as the Cundy Graves at Curbar, which date from 1632 and the Riley Graves (which contain the Hancock family) at Eyam. The Eyam plague dates from 1665-6. A further, little known, group of gravestones attributed to this plague exists at the old Bretton Farm, now a youth hostel. They were apparently victims from the families of Morton, Hall and Townsend at Bretton. There is a further group situated near to the Bow Stones, south of Lyme Hall in the west of the Peak. These relate to the victims of a plague which swept the area in 1646, but most of the stones have now been removed. The surviving stones are difficult to find and not on a public footpath, being situated north of the Bow Stones.

44 Cundy Graves, Curbar

45 Riley Graves, Eyam

In the days before today's preventative medicines, disease was far more common and occasional pitiful stories of the plague and its consequences survive. Eyam is perhaps the best known example, because of the terrible toll in human misery when 257 people died. Affected communities still needed to live and work however. Food and other provisions would be left at a certain spot and the money for payment left in vinegar, ostensibly to purify it. Such places were often marked by a stone and at least two plague stones remain near the Peak together with a well which used to contain the vinegar at Eyam. These are shown in photographs 46, 47 and 48.

46   Mompesson's Well, Eyam

47   Plague stone at
         Birchall, Leek

— 33 —

48   The Dipping Stone at Whaley Moor, Whaley Bridge

49   Hospitals for the working classes became widespread during the nineteenth century. Buxton Hospital had been built between 1785-90 as a stable block for the hotel patrons at The Crescent. In 1859, it was converted to the Devonshire Royal Hospital 'for the use of the sick poor'. The building had a circular courtyard with a colonnade supported by large Tuscan columns. Here horses were exercised when it was a stable. In 1881, this courtyard was covered by a dome, 156ft in diameter. At the time it was the largest unsupported dome in the world, weighing 560 tons. Today, it must be one of very few hospitals open to outside visitors and selling a guide book as a souvenir.

50 The field patterns now preserved by countless stone walls often retain the outline of farming techniques of long ago. At Royston Grange, north-east of Ashbourne, some of the walls are considered to date from Roman times. Many of the walls are on the boundaries of strips from the old strip system of farming. One field, shown here, between Hartington and Biggin and near Heathcote Mere is two strips wide, both strips being in occupation before the walls were built and appearing on William Senior's plan of the Chatsworth estate dated 1614.

51 Various narrow strips were amalgamated at Longnor and they can be clearly seen on this photograph.

52   Chelmorton (above) is well known for visual reminders of its past. Not only are there the numerous walls which marked the consolidation of the narrow strip system into slightly larger units, but at the inner, village end of the strips, the new owners built their houses creating the elongated pattern of the village which we can see today.

53   A fascinating example of the old strip system exists in the ridge and furrow marks which survive alongside the A515 at Tissington. The characteristic ridge and furrow profile comes from ploughing in different directions, throwing the soil over towards the middle of the strip. The plough-man turned his horse around at the end of the strip giving the 's' shape seen below.

54   The valley of the Manifold contains some good examples of strip lynchets — although they are no means confined to this area. Experts seem to have differing opinions on the age of these terraces which were used for agricultural purposes. This group is situated to the west of Throwley Hall and can be clearly seen as a group of parallel lines in the middle of the photograph. They could easily be a thousand years or even much older in age.

55   These dovecotes may be seen in the gable end of Knowsley Cross Farm near Longnor. Doves were formerly an important source of meat, especially in medieval times.

56 The remaining part of the medieval Padley Hall at Grindleford is the old gate house and chapel which also has a dovecote in the gable end, seen here (left).

57 The stone tank shown below was built in 1829 and is known as The Fountain. It provided a head of water for Youlgreave village, the supply coming from the south of Bradford Dale. The supply is still in use to this day, the villagers having the advantage of a water supply considerably cheaper than that provided by the Severn Trent Water Board. The capacity of the tank is 1,200 gallons. It is 9ft high and 9ft in diameter, but no longer used.

Stocks and Lock-Ups

There is no way of knowing how many villages and surrounding towns had a lock-up or stocks. It is clear that some have been lost; at Monyash, for example, the village cross is supposedly standing on the stone sides of the old village stocks. However a few remain, some restored with recent woodwork. Here is what is hoped is a comprehensive list, and includes, for completeness, villages surrounding the Peak: Birchover; Bolsterstone; Chapel-en-le-Frith; Cheddleton; Eyam; Litton; Mottram; Rainow; High Bradfield; Warslow; Wormhill.

58   Birchover stocks, situated to the south of the village on the old lane to Winster, at SK 240618. Restored.

59   Bolsterstone. Almost hidden behind the railings, this set of stocks is situated against the churchyard wall.

60 Chapel-en-le-Frith. Stocks in the market square.

61 Cheddleton. Opposite the Black Lion Inn can be seen the cast-iron stocks set into the churchyard wall. They have been damaged since this photograph was taken.

62 Eyam. A photograph taken of the hall about a century ago (and reproduced in *The Peak District: Pictures from the Past*) shows the stone sides of the stocks but with no wooden rails which must have been subsequently replaced.

63 Litton. Situated outside the village pub, this set would have been ideally placed as a reminder against excessive drinking!

64   Mottram. Although an expanding town on the outskirts of Greater Manchester, the heart of the town still has a village feel about it. Opposite the old Court House (now the information centre) can be seen the stocks, moved to this site a few years ago.

65   Rainow. Just below the A5002 close to the boundary sign of the National Park can be found these stocks in Stocks Lane.

66 High Bradfield. This set is situated on the road northwards out of the village and close to the pub.

67 Warslow. These cast iron stocks are situated where the lane to Ivy House Farm leaves the main road, close to the school.

68 Wormhill. These are to be found on the grass surround to the memorial to James Brindley.

69 This is Hayfield lock-up, built in 1799, when it was referred to as the 'New Prison'. It is situated in Market Street on the left of a small square known as Dungeon Brow. The stocks in front of the building appear to be new. The upstairs room has its own door to the square and was built as the Parish Council's Committee room. It is still used for this purpose.

70 Lock-ups are more rare and were really places of temporary confinement pending transfer to more permanent gaols. One also suspects that many a drunk may have slept it off in them too, prior to release the following morning! This small building in Cromford had two cells and is now preserved. It is behind the main street, just to the east of North Street.

71 This is the lock-up at Alton, which survives by the side of the road to Denstone. Although not strictly in the Peak, it is included as it seems to have been very similar to one that formerly existed in Longnor, on the road to Glutton. A photograph of the latter fortunately survives and is reproduced in *Bygone Days in the Peak District*.

72 This unusual building is at Curbar, just downhill from the Cundy Graves. Clarence Daniel (*Derbyshire Life*, Volume 17, No 3, 1948) asserts that it was built as a Bath House to Cliff College nearby. It does however appear to have been used as a lock-up for a short period and later used as a dwelling house until 1935 when it was condemned. The construction of the roof is fascinating, flat slabs receding one above the other to reach the apex.

73   In addition to confinement, another old punishment for 'scolds' was the ducking stool. This chair at Leek parish church is traditionally held to have been one and to have been used in the local River Churnet! Even if you, like me, find it difficult to believe the story, one has to agree it is intriguing, especially because of the hole in the back!

Churches and Crosses

Many of the Peak's churches date from medieval times but were often 'restored' by the Victorians, although one suspects that the sometimes drastic alterations may often have been dictated by structural decay. Certainly, Bakewell, Parwich and Warslow (strictly speaking pre-Victorian) fall into this category.

Many churches have features of interest and a few are highlighted here. Two chapels are also included which contrast greatly with each other. They are the resplendent Chatsworth chapel and the older Haddon Hall chapel. The latter is still the parish church of Nether Haddon, but such niceties pale against the simple beauty of this Norman building with its medieval wall paintings, now in danger of being lost. Pre-Norman remains exist in some unusual guises and some of these are featured too. Many of our local Peakland churches need the financial support of visitors and one hopes that this chapter helps to draw attention to both our heritage and the need to dig deep into our pockets to help maintain it.

74   There are many pre-Reformation monuments and brasses in the fourteenth-century church at Tideswell (above), considered to be one of the finest churches in Derbyshire. It includes a brass showing Bishop Pursglove of Hull, a native of Tideswell, in full Eucharistic vestments as worn prior to the Reformation. It dates from 1579. The church has much else of interest, including some old and interesting pews.

75 Jenkin Chapel dates from 1733, the tower being added in 1755. It is a most unusual building, looking more like an adapted dwelling house than a chapel. Even the original interior has a homely feel about it with its small size and box pews. It was built alongside an important saltway. Just to the south of the chapel is Saltersford Hall, a reminder of the days when packhorses carrying their loads of salt from the Cheshire 'wiches' would be a regular sight.

An open-air service is held here on the second Sunday in September at 3pm.

76 To the south of Jenkin Chapel lies Macclesfield Forest. Here, the old Forest Chapel survives. A low simple building of no great architectural distinction, it is, however, well known for its Rush Bearing Service. On the nearest Sunday to 12 August, the church floor is strewn with rushes and a service is held in the afternoon, attended by many people. In the large field to the south-west of the chapel and north of the road to Langley is an earthwork, roughly rectangular in shape, consisting of a rampart and a ditch. Excavations have revealed the foundations of a building now considered to be the original hunting lodge of the old forest. The old packhorse road which passed the church can be seen behind the church in this photograph.

77   Padley Chapel, situated near Grindleford Railway Station is the sole remnant of Padley Hall, built in the fourteenth and fifteenth centuries. The Fitzherberts who lived at the hall were Catholics and two Catholic priests were arrested here in 1588. They were convicted, hung, drawn and quartered at Derby. The chapel fell into disuse but was restored in 1933. A service of remembrance for the 'Padley Martyrs' is held annually on the Thursday nearest 12 July. Behind the chapel are the excavated remains of the hall itself.

78   The barn at Alport Castles Farm, was first used in 1662 for Nonconformist worship. It was ideally situated at the head of Alport Dale, west of Ladybower Reservoir. Today, an annual 'Love Feast' is held here on the first Sunday in July (details from The Manse, Hathersage).

79 Robin Hood's companion, John Little, better known as Little John was a nail maker in Hathersage. He lived in a cottage near to the church and his grave is near the south porch. Whether one believes the story or not, it is nonetheless gratifying to have this link with 'Merrie England'.

80 This curious inscription, 'James Robinson interred February the 28th 1788 Aged 438', can be found in the churchyard of St Edward the Confessor, at Leek, close to the tower door! On the north side of the church in a graveyard on the hillside are many graves of Napoleonic prisoners of war who lived in houses adjacent. The area is still known as 'Petty France'. The church has two lovely thirteenth-century rose windows.

81 This grave is situated in Longnor churchyard in North Staffordshire and the epitaph is reproduced in full: 'In memory of William Billinge, who was born in a Cornfield at Fawfieldhead, in this Parish, in the Year 1679. At the age of 23 years he enlisted into His Majesty's Service under Sir George Rooke, and was at the taking of the Fortress of Gibralter, in 1704. He afterwards served under the Duke of Marlborough at the ever Memorable Battle of Ramilles, on the 23rd of May, 1706, where he was wounded by a musket shot in the thigh. He afterwards returned to his native country, and with manly courage defended his Sovereign's rights at the Rebellion in 1715 and 1745. He died within a space of 150 yards of where he was born and was interred here the 30th of January 1791 aged 112 years — Billited by Death, I quartered here remain. When the trumpet sounds, I'll rise and march again'.

82 Another case of longevity can be seen at Wirksworth church, close to the south porch where Matthew Peat lies buried. He died on 11 December 1757, aged 109 years and 10 months. Few would argue with his epitaph 'few live so long'.

83 This is a 'Watch House' built to deter bodysnatchers from the churchyard at High Bradfield church. Its occupier would act as a caretaker for the churchyard.

84 Maiden's gloves or paper garlands were hung in churches if a girl died before marriage. Shakespeare referred to them as 'virgin crants' in the funeral scene of Ophelia in *Hamlet*. Examples can be seen in Ashford, Matlock and Ilam churches. These are at Ilam.

85   There are, as one may expect, many memorials in the churches of the Peak District, including some fine examples of early monuments, the seventeenth-century alabaster monument to the Bassett family at Blore being one of the largest. Of the later monuments, two are portrayed here, arguably amongst the finest in the region. This marble memorial to David Pike Watts by Francis L. Chantrey is at Ilam. It dates from 1826 and rests in a private chapel built in 1831. It is one of Chantrey's best carvings, possibly only surpassed by his carving at Lichfield Cathedral of the Robinson children in the South Choir Aisle.

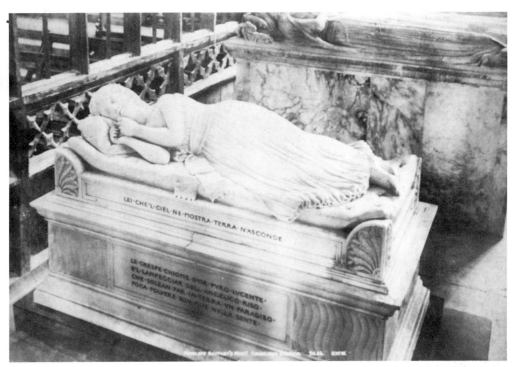

86   The Boothby Chapel at Ashbourne has a considerable number of memorials, but it is best known for the marble carving of Penelope Boothby. It was carved by Thomas Banks in 1793 and is his most famous work. An inscription reads 'She was in form and intellect most exquisite. The unfortunate Parents ventured their all on this frail bark. And the wreck was total.' The memorial was exhibited at the Royal Academy and Queen Charlotte supposedly wept when she saw it.

87   The Peak is well endowed with early churchyard crosses, although many of them are fragments of larger crosses. Only one has an original head (Eyam) and even here, a section of the shaft is missing. This beautifully carved cross is possibly early ninth century, with coarse vine scrolls and interlace work.

88   This is Stile House Cross, taking its name from a nearby farm. It is situated on Morridge, east of Leek and stands in a field. It was probably a preaching cross for the Bradnop Quarter of the old Leek Parish, as another cross (now gone) on Gun Hill was used for a similar purpose in the Frith Quarter, north of Leek. A further one exists south of Leek at Basford in the Cheddleton Quarter which is similar in shape. A reference in the church register for 1666 refers to the Bradnop Quarter church warden spending time 'att ye side of Morridge'. This could well have been at this cross.

89   Hope Churchyard Cross (not to be confused with Hope Cross). It is probably eleventh century with interlace work and pairs of figures, one set apparently carrying a cross.

90-2 Ilam. The church has two crosses, the upper section of a round-shafted cross (opposite, top) and a rectangular one (below), both near the south porch. A further cross, popularly known as the 'Battle Cross' — a piece of Victorian romanticism — can be seen in Paradise Walk, in the grounds of the Hall (opposite, bottom). It was rescued from a cottage when the village was rebuilt.

93-4 Bakewell church possesses the largest collection of medieval monuments in the United Kingdom. They are grave covers (or parts of them) which were found during restoration work in 1841-2 (below). Some of the stones are earlier and of Anglo-Saxon date. They are to be seen in the south porch and in the west wall of the nave. They were presumably originally parts of coffin lids that were used in the fabric of a later church. Other coffin lids are to be found built into the fabric of Baslow church nearby, but these are rather too high for close inspection. In the photograph below are several stone coffins which are propped up against the side of the south porch. There must have been many more, judging by the numerous parts of the stone coffin lids. In Bakewell churchyard are two crosses, of the ninth and eleventh centuries. The one beneath the eastern end of the church came from Two Dales, near Matlock and is shown here (left).

95   Near the abandoned ruins of Errwood
Hall, in the Goyt Valley, is this private
burial ground of the Grimshawe family, who
built the house in the early part of the
nineteenth century. It contains the remains
of members of the family and their servants
including the captain of their yacht, *Mar-
quita.*

96   Behind Errwood Hall, on the moor is
the circular stone-built shrine to Miss
Dolores, a Spanish companion to Mrs
Grimshawe and governess to the children. It
was built in 1889 and is still available for a
few moment's quiet contemplation.

97 Perhaps the oldest chapel in the Peak is the one at Haddon Hall. It was originally the parish church of Nether Haddon and Pevsner attributes the west and south walls to the twelfth century. The chancel dates from 1427. The hall was carefully restored earlier this century and the wonderful wall paintings were revealed. They include St Christopher standing in water with numerous fish and plants, together with woodland scenes and traces of the original paintwork. The only modern addition is the beautiful memorial to Robert Charles John Manners, Lord Haddon, who died in 1894, aged nine.

98 The most beautiful chapel, endowed without apparent regard to cost is the one at Chatsworth, although the volume of visitors can often preclude a quiet moment's reflection here. It was built between 1688 and 1693 and remains unaltered. The reredos or altar-piece is carved from local alabaster with black columns carved from Ashford black marble. The large painting above the altar is by Verrio and shows 'Doubting Thomas'. The carvings either side of this showing Faith and Justice are by Cibber.

The walls are of cedar wood and the limewood carvings are by Samuel Watson who also was responsible for the altar-piece. Laguerre's paintings on the walls and ceiling complete the scene.

On the Road

The Peak has a fascinating network of early road systems, including several old roads which run for miles and are now abandoned. The bleak moorlands of the north are particularly important in this respect. Many of these old roads survive and now carry motor vehicles, while others are the preserve of the rambler. There are some interesting remains of these old roads: wayside crosses and milestones apparently in the middle of nowhere, packhorse bridges, abandoned bridges, snowstones and so on. They all combine to add to the heritage of the region.

99-100   The age of this superb packhorse bridge at Three Shires Head is unknown. It is clear from looking underneath (opposite) that it has been widened, probably to enable carts to get from Cut Thorn Hill in Cheshire to Dane Head and Flash Bar. Four distinct packhorse routes meet at this bridge, which is known to this day as Pannier's Pool Bridge, after the panniers carried by the horses. The old trade routes now make very good footpaths and all are recommended for getting to know this quiet part of the Peak.

101 One path from Three Shires Head goes via Flash Bar to Longnor and Hollinsclough. The latter was the home of John Lomas (1747-1823), a jaggerman or packhorse man. He prospered at his trade and built this chapel in the garden of his house in 1801. The chapel was being re-roofed when this photograph was taken.

102 Another path from Three Shires Head descends the Dane Valley and at Gradbach it is crossed by a packhorse route from Wildboarclough to Gradbach Mill. An inn was built at this crossing in 1738 and was known as The Eagle and Child. It is no longer a pub but the sign remains and in the porch there is a motif of an eagle carrying a child. It is now a private home but carries on the refreshment tradition by selling afternoon tea. The eagle and child are taken from the badge of the Stanley family (the Lords of Derby) who have an estate at Wildboarclough.

103   This is the Holme Bridge, a narrow packhorse bridge, on the River Wye at Bakewell. Structures like this were very important and stone bridges exist from medieval times. This one was built later in 1664. Matlock bridge dates from the thirteenth century, although it has been rebuilt several times.

104   Hanging Bridge over the River Dove, Mayfield, west of Ashbourne dated from medieval times and the original structure still exists despite widening in 1937. The original arches can be seen in this picture.

105   Upstream of Hanging Bridge, on the River Dove is Coldwall Bridge, now abandoned. Roads radiated away from the Peak District and this old road was turnpiked in 1762 and ran from Thorpe to Blythe Marsh near the Potteries. The road was built to carry coal and lime. It was also used to help transport blocks of chert from mines near Bakewell to the Potteries, where they were used to grind flint — an essential ingredient in the making of fine china. The bridge was built in 1726 and now lies unused, although the road from Thorpe is still surfaced. The bridge replaced a wooden bridge and when built was 9ft wide. It was subsequently doubled in width which would seem to indicate it was formerly used by considerable traffic.

106   On the Thorpe side of Coldwall Bridge is a milestone set up in 1822 (below). It reads 'Cheadle 11'.

107 A much older road is Doctor's Gate, Snake Pass. Here it can be seen crossing Coldharbour Moor. It is a Roman road and its cobbled surface complete with curbstones survives. Its name comes from Doctor Talbot, illegitimate son of the Earl of Shrewsbury. He was vicar of Glossop from 1494 to 1550 and must have often used the road as he travelled between Glossop and Sheffield Castle, owned by his father.

108 This roadway is the packhorse road at Washgate Bridge, a short distance below the source of the River Dove. It is one of the best examples of a metalled packhorse road to have survived in the Peak.

109   Another unused roadway is this piece of the 1759 turnpike road near The Cat and Fiddle Inn on the Buxton-Macclesfield road. It dates from 1759 and is known as 'Stoney-way'. It retains its original surface, which is of interest. The milestone is inscribed 'To Macclesfield 6 miles' and 'To London 164 miles'. The road was re-routed in 1823 to its current alignment which accounts for the abandonment of this particular section. Note the low earth banks with 30ft of roadway between them.

110   The Cat and Fiddle Inn is one of many throughout the Peak built to meet the needs of travellers in the turnpike era. It was described as 'newly erected' in 1831. It is currently the highest inn in England with a 7-day licence. Here is a view of it in the days of the stage coach.

111   Ten years prior to the construction of the Cat and Fiddle Inn, another of the Peak's best known inns was built and was called Lady Clough House. Its name was soon changed to the Snake Inn, after the Duke of Devonshire, whose crest includes a snake. Today, now called the Snake Pass Inn, it stands at the side of the Snake Road. The latter reaches the top of the Snake Pass at a height of 1,680ft, where it is crossed by the Pennine Way. It was formerly one of the highest turnpike roads in England.

112   This is The Strines Inn, at the western end of Bradfield Dale. There has been a building here since 1275. In the sixteenth century, the Worrall family lived here and their coat of arms may be seen over the doorway.

113 Above the Strines Inn, at the top of the steep slope down to the Strines Brook is this stone with the inscription 'Take off'. It is understood to be a marker where additional horses used on the climb up the road were unharnessed. It can be found by the telegraph pole.

114 This mounting block exists in Hartington village and was used to mount horses. It is situated outside The Old Vicarage in Church Street. This house was built in the eighteenth century for Cornelius Flint, the Duke of Devonshire's agent at the Ecton Copper Mine from 1779 to about 1811. A well inside the house is lined with stone, typical of many mine shafts in the area.

115 This old guide stone is a well preserved example and can be seen near the Bar Brook on Big Moor. It is on the Chesterfield-Curbar road and can be seen to the Chesterfield side of its junction with the A621 Baslow-Owler Bar road. The inscription reads 'To Chesterfield 7 miles / Tideswell 9 miles, Manchester 36 miles'. Just upstream on the Bar Brook from this junction is a clapper bridge dated 1742. The current straight alignment of the road occurred 17 years later when the road was turnpiked in 1759.

116 At the top of Curbar Gap stands this guidepost (below), marking the way for travellers in times gone by. If you look carefully over the wall, you can see what looks like the line of the old highway running slightly to the north of the existing roadway.

117   In the limestone areas, surface water for animals is uncommon. It was (and still is) a valuable commodity. Rainwater was therefore retained in clay lined ponds called 'meres'. Some are of a considerable age. There is documentary evidence of Heathcote Mere (pictured here) existing in 1482. It is also shown on a Chatsworth estate map of the Hartington area dated 1614, which incidentally, does not show the one in the centre of Hartington village nearby.

118   Roadside evidence of past industry can be seen at Holme. On the right hand side of the road to Digley Reservoir are twenty-five pairs of holes in the wall. These held tenter-hooks, used for drying yarns.

119 This stone was once described to me by an old local farmer as being a 'bargain stone'. Men shook hands through the stone to strike a deal. If this is so, it has surely been moved to its present situation at SK 097604, north of Hulme End. It is now a gate post.

120 A similar fate has happened to this guide post at SK 238597 south of Winster. It indicates the way to 'Bakewell/Bonsall/ Worksworth [sic]/Leeke [sic]'. It indicates the way from the end of Bonsall Lane, a little to the north of its current position.

121 Wayside crosses survive across the Peak in varying degrees of completeness and varying antiquity. This is Edale Cross. It stands to the west of Jacob's Ladder near the point where three wards of the former Royal Forest of the Peak met. They were Longdendale, Ashop and Edale, and Champayne. The cross bears the date 1810, but this marks the date of its restoration. The footpath here is an old medieval road from Hayfield to Edale.

122 Further east, there was another cross of similar age called Eccles Cross. A further one, which does survive on the road between the Edale Valley and the Derwent Valley is Hope Cross (pictured). Today it has a capstone dated 1737.

123   In the west of the Peak, this is probably the socketed base of a medieval cross. It is known as the Abbot's Chair and is situated on the Monk's Road near The Grouse Inn on the Glossop-Hayfield road, at SK 029904. It has had this name since at least 1640. Basingwerk Abbey, in Flintshire owned land here. It was given to them in 1157 by Henry II and parts of the road were paved as early as 1290.

124   Cleulow Cross near Wincle can just be seen between the trees on top of the hill in this picture (below). It was a landmark on the old medieval road between Leek and Macclesfield. The road is in an old holloway which passes just to the west of the cross. This area of the western peak has other crosses whose exact function is now unclear.

125 The Bow Stones are considered to be Saxon and possibly the base of two crosses, the shafts of which are preserved at Lyme Hall. They are similar to the Robin Hood's Picking Rods and both may have been important landmarks as well as having a possible religious significance. The Bow Stones, south of Lyme Park, at SK 973813 are worth seeking out if only for the magnificent view.

126 To visit Robin Hood's Picking Rods, park on the Monk's Road, between Glossop and Hayfield at Plainsteads (SK 024910) and walk over Cown Edge Rocks. The stones are on the path which is a packhorse way — at SK 006909.

127   Wayside markers in the Peak tend to be referred to as crosses, probably because the earlier examples, such as Cleulow Cross, were probably erected by monks. In the case of Cleulow Cross, the monks of Dieulacresse Abbey near Leek would be regular users of the Macclesfield road and the Monk's Road near the Abbot's Chair has also been mentioned above. Consequently it comes as no surprise to learn that this exposed eighteenth-century way-mark stone on Ipstones Edge is called Windy Harbor Cross. It stands on the road used by pack-horses to carry copper ore from Ecton Mine, near Warslow to Whiston near the Churnet Valley in Staffordshire.

128   These two stones are snow-stones, marking the edge of the road between Longnor and the Leek-Buxton road. There are four of them in all, with a possible fifth now used as a gatepost.

129 This is Knowsley Cross on the Longnor-Sheen road, an old ridge road between the Rivers Dove and Manifold. This cross was restored in 1899 and although roughly hewn it seems well preserved.

130 The south-western corner of the Peak has several examples of an unusual type of stile. Here is one of them (below). It adequately allows the passage of people but not sheep and cattle. This example is on the Buxton-Ashbourne road, just south of Newhaven, looking towards the Tissington Trail and is of very fine workmanship considering its mundane purpose.

131 This is all that remains of the bridge chapel that existed by the bridge over the Derwent at Cromford. Both the chapel and bridge date from the fifteenth century.

132 On the side of the road on Whaley Moor above Whaley Bridge, by the old road to Disley is a reminder that it could be dangerous on the road — this stone tells us that here was murdered William Wood of Eyam on 16 July 1823.

133-4   This stone exists to the north of Lamaload Reservoir near Rainow. It is marked as 'memorial stone' on the White Peak ordnance map. The inscription reads — 'Here John Turner was cast away in a heavy snow storm in the night in or about the year 1755.' On the reverse side it reads 'The print of a woman's shoe was found by his side in the snow were [sic] he lay dead'. How intriguing!

Canals and Railways

Although the Peak did not have many railways and its canals only reached the periphery of the area, they did have some unusual features. The earliest railway line in the area was the Cromford and High Peak Railway, which was started in 1825 (the year the Stockton and Darlington Railway opened), was opened five years later and used horses on the level sections until 1850, when steam locomotives were introduced. There were eight long inclines which initially had stationary steam engines to haul up the rolling stock. The Manifold Valley Light Railway was modelled on an Indian line — the Barsi Light Railway — and ran on a 30in gauge. Not all lines are included here; the Ashover Light Railway and the long Froghall

incline are excluded, as are the several mineral inclines and lines of the Churnet Valley. However some major remains of lines in the Péak are included and these are likely to be of more general interest. The canals are now chiefly pleasant waterways for walking and other recreational activities. Perhaps the rarest feature on the canals is the preserved steam driven beam engine working a huge plunger pump at Leawood near Cromford. This immense engine, which is steamed each year on several dates, is a unique survivor.

135 This cast iron mile post at Froghall Wharf on the Caldon Canal is a recent replacement, although an original one exists at Cheddleton. It reminds us that the canal originally ran as far as Uttoxeter, the extension from Froghall opening in 1811. The extension was however, uneconomic and closed in the 1840s.

136 The Caldon Canal was taken over by the North Staffordshire Railway, who ran their line down the side of the canal. Consall station was even cantilevered out over the canal. A reminder of these days may still be seen outside the Black Lion Inn at Consall Forge. This stone marks the boundary of the railway company's land. The inn was a canal pub and today is popular with canal users and ramblers.

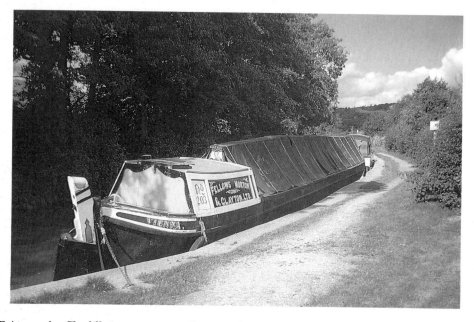

137 At nearby Cheddleton, a preserved narrow boat *Vienna* lies moored adjacent to the flint mill wharf. It serves as a reminder of a way of life which has now passed into history.

138   The Caldon Canal has a branch to Leek at Denford. The Leek arm crosses over the Froghall branch on a large stone and brick aqueduct (pictured). From here, one can walk westwards for about a mile to where the two branches join at Denford Locks. The latter were built in 1842 with side ponds. These, together with a rather nice cast-iron bridge, present a good subject for photographers and canal enthusiasts.

139   The Caldon Canal is fed with water from Rudyard Lake which draws on the River Dane. The supply channel is known as 'The Feeder', and commences at Gig Hall Bridge (pictured). The River Dane flows eventually to the Irish Sea via the River Weaver. 'The Feeder' feeds the Caldon Canal which shares a common course with the River Churnet at Consall Forge. This water finds its way to the North Sea via the River Trent! Currently the River Dane end of 'The Feeder' is kept empty but it's a lovely walk in any event.

140   The Caldon Canal was engineered by James Brindley, who was born in 1716 at Tunstead to the west of Tideswell. A memorial to him exists at Wormhill nearby (above).

141   Brindley designed the Leek Corn Mill in 1752. Today it is open to the public and the top floor has a museum devoted to him.

142   Brindley's family had moved to Leek in 1726 and in 1733 he was apprenticed to Abraham Bennett of Sutton, near Macclesfield. Bennett's house and workshop still survives and a plaque records its historical connection.

143   While an apprentice, Brindley established his reputation as a genius during the construction of Lower Crag Mill at Wildboarclough. Bennett proved himself incompetent and the mill was engineered by Brindley in 1737. It was demolished in 1958 and only this small piece of wall remains. Remains of walls can, however, be seen in the trees planted on the mill site.

144 The Cromford Canal was built in 1790 and although it is no longer connected with Nottingham (through a tunnel collapse) there is much of interest to see. The canal connected with the Cromford and High Peak Railway and many relics of this ancient railway (opened in 1830-1) remain. These include the maintenance shed — which is open to the public — with an inspection pit with 'C & HPR' cast on the rails either side. It is claimed that the short length of 'fish belly' line each side of the inspection pit is the oldest *in situ* piece of railway line in the world.

145 A little way up the Sheep Pasture incline is the incline catchpit, built to catch runaway wagons. It was put to good use as the illustration shows; the wagon remains to this day having crashed in September 1965.

146 The Cromford and High Peak Railway united the Cromford Canal with the Peak Forest Canal. The top section of the latter — from Whaley Bridge to Marple — was opened in 1800 and is one of the highest lengths of navigable water in England. At Marple there is a remarkable series of sixteen locks which enables the canal to descend 208ft. Here are two of the locks between Marple Bridge and Marple Aqueduct.

147 The canal crossed the River Goyt by the Marple Aqueduct. It was built by Benjamin Outram who had worked on the Cromford Canal with William Jessop. It is 90ft high. Either side of the arches, the masonry is pierced by circular holes to lessen the weight of the structure. Fifty or so years later it was joined by the adjacent railway viaduct.

148 Between Middleton Top and Parsley Hay Wharf, where the lines from Ashbourne and Cromford united, there were two features unique in the whole railway system of the country. At Hopton was the steepest incline worked without assistance with a gradient of 1:14. Originally the rolling stock was hauled up the incline by a stationary engine, similar to the one at Middleton Top. Here is shown an old photograph with an engine on the incline.

149 Hopton incline today

150 Secondly, at Gotham near Pikelow was the tightest curve on the whole national railway system, with a radius of $2^1/_2$ chains. This can be found by parking at Minninglow Wharf north of Parwich and walking westwards.

151 If you walk in the opposite direction from Minninglow Wharf, ie eastwards, you soon start to cross a huge embankment with another one visible around a bend in the line below Minninglow itself.

152 At the tunnel which carries the A515 over the railway near Parsley Hay may be seen two plaques, one at each end. The plaque at the northern end is shown here. It shows a wagon and the Latin motto *Divina Palladis Arte* ('By the Divine Skill of Pallas' or Minerva, the Greek god of engineering). This is surrounded by the inscription 'Cromford and High Peak Railway Compy Incorporated 1825'. It is accompanied by the names of Josias Jessop, the line's engineer and Wm Brittlebank, the company solicitor.

153 There were two other railways in the south-west of the Peak in addition to the Cromford and High Peak Railway — the Buxton to Ashbourne line, built in 1890 and the Manifold Valley Light Railway opened in 1904. The signal box at Hartington station survives as an information centre and is more or less complete.

154 At Hulme End Station, on the Manifold Valley Light Railway, two of the three principal buildings of the former light railway survive, even though it closed in 1934 and the buildings are of temporary materials (chiefly wood and corrugated iron). The building on the left was the booking office and the larger building was the engine shed. The station opened in 1904 a few years after Hartington Station. None the less, it was known as 'Hulme End — for Sheen and Hartington'. Today the site is a maintenance depot. How enterprising it would be if the latter was moved along the site a little and the buildings used as an interpretative centre for the old railway.

155 Matlock had the steepest gradient cable tramway in the world. It ran up Bank Road from Crown Square from March 1893 until 1927 and had a gradient of $1:5^1/_2$. At the top of Bank Road is Rutland Street where the Tram Depot (illustrated above) still remains. It was built in 1893.

156 Although Matlock had the only tram system in the Peak District, the demise of the tram across the country resulted in a renaissance of the tram in the Peak, with the establishment of the National Tramway Museum in Crich. The museum restores old trams and has re-established much tram memorabilia on its site. Whether it's fine or wet, it's always a good day out at Crich!

157 Stationary steam engines are rare in the Peak, but two survivors are near to each other and happily open to the public at certain times. Leawood Pumphouse was built to supply the Cromford Canal with water from the River Derwent. The engine was built on the Cornish principle and has a huge cylinder of 50in diameter. It was built in 1849 at Milton Works, Elsecar, Yorkshire. There are occasional steam days when it is well worth going to see it. It is the largest plunger pump surviving in the country and pumps 4 tons of water at each stroke.

158-9 The other engine is at Middleton Top and was used to haul railway engines and wagons up the Middleton incline of the Cromford and High Peak Railway. It has two much smaller cylinders working a huge fly wheel.

160-1   There was a considerable outcry when Monsal Viaduct was built in 1860, although it was probably the scarring of the valley up river which created the main outcry rather than the bridge itself. Today, it enhances the view of Monsal Dale and the scars of the railway cuttings have largely grassed over.

A rare view of this bridge actually being built can be seen in *The Peak District: Pictures from the Past*. Here are two views showing the valley with its bridge and a close up of the structure.

At Work

The character of work has changed over the years. Even agriculture — never an industry to show rapid change in any event — has altered in terms of techniques, amount of labour employed etc. Many industries have gone altogether and all we have now are the remains of past endeavours. Some fall readily into the category of the curious; incomplete stone troughs, millstones abandoned on the eastern edges, aqueduct piers in Lathkill Dale etc, spring readily to mind. The illustrations in this chapter include examples of old mills, limekilns and mines. They are not comprehensive and many other examples may be found without much difficulty, such as Edale cotton mill, now converted to flats. The limekilns and mines, by their very nature are potentially dangerous places and should be treated as such.

62 Perhaps the most ancient industry in the area, other than agriculture of course, is lead mining. A Roman presence in this respect is known because of several Roman pigs of lead which have been found. A Roman smelting centre is thought to have existed, called *Lutudarum*. Excavations at Carsington on land which will be inundated under the new reservoir have unearthed a villa site, two pigs of lead and evidence of smelting. A further pig of lead was discovered nearby sometime ago. It is to be hoped that the actual site will not be lost beneath the waters. Bonsall has seen considerable mining activity and this Saxon carving of a lead miner was found there in 1870. It can now be seen in the south transept of Wirksworth church.

163 The Odin Mine at Castleton is traditionally held to be one of the oldest workings and its name may well have been an indicator of this. No documentary evidence survives to prove this, however. It lies below the Blue John Mine and this crushing stone with its iron crushing ring survives close to the road. A further crushing stone may be seen at the mining display area at the Crich Tramway Museum.

164 One of the main mining areas was known as 'The King's Field' and it had, indeed still has, its own mining rules, now formalised in two Acts of Parliament. The governing body of 'The King's Field' is the Barmoot Court which still meets. It is the oldest industrial court in Britain and may have been in existence for the best part of a thousand years. It meets at the Moot Hall in Wirksworth (pictured). The jury of twenty-four people still receive a clay pipe, tobacco and a meal just as its predecessors have done for centuries.

165 An example of an old engine house (similar to those commonly found in Cornwall) is at Mandale Mine in Lathkill Dale. It was built in 1847 but closed in 1851.

166 A little upstream from the mine are the stone pillars of an aqueduct, built in 1840 which supplied water to a waterwheel adjacent to the engine house remains. A nineteenth-century view of the aqueduct can be seen in illustration 99 of *The Peak District: Pictures from the Past.*

167 The nineteenth century saw much activity and investment in Derbyshire's lead mines. Many of the mine buildings have been razed to the ground, but an exception is Magpie Mine, near to Sheldon, where buildings, chimneys and even some of the machinery still survives. The main shaft is 600ft deep and the mine has a 3-mile-long drainage level or sough to the River Wye at Shacklow Wood. The mine only closed in 1958 and is a fascinating insight into the history of a compact lead mine over 150 years.

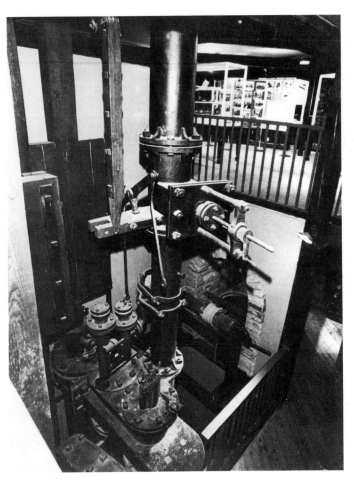

168 Many relics of the lead mining era have been gathered together and may be seen in the country's only museum solely devoted to the subject. It is situated at the Peak District Mining Museum at the Pavilion, Matlock Bath and even includes mock passages and a shaft which are very popular with children. The main exhibit is a huge engine dated 1819 which was found in a mine near Winster. It used water instead of steam for pressure and is a unique survivor in this country.

169 If you fancy a trip down an old mine, three are open for you to choose from. All are abandoned mines now run as tourist attractions. They are: Good Luck Mine, Via Gellia; Temple Mine, Matlock Bath; and Holme Bank Chert Mine, Bakewell. Details of all three can be obtained from the Peak District Mining Museum (☎ Matlock 3834). Illustrated is the entrance to Holme Bank Chert Mine.

170 The millstone grit in the Hathersage area has long been used for the manufacture of grind stones or millstones — so much so that the geological name reflects its former importance. Near Surprise View a footpath leaves the road by a National Trust sign marked 'Bole Hill Quarry'. The path is actually an old railway track, which connected to the main line by a steep incline and hundreds of abandoned millstones still lie stacked in rows. Elsewhere one stumbles across isolated examples where a convenient piece of stone was cut and perhaps cracked during carving.

171   In sight of Carl Wark is also this trough lying abandoned and incomplete, possibly because it had cracked.

172   Only one watermill survives as a museum in the National Park itself and that is Caudwell's Cornmill at Rowsley where turbines drive the rollers in the mill.

173-4 However, even Caudwell's Cornmill does not have any waterwheels and one has to look to the periphery of the Peak to find mills (complete with wheels) which are open to the public. Cheddleton Flint Mill is situated beside the River Churnet and the Caldon Canal. It has two wheels facing each other, which is most unusual. It also has a preserved narrow boat — *Vienna* (see Fig 137) — moored on the canal. The mill is open at weekends.

175 The Peak Forest Canal extended to Whaley Bridge (to receive the traffic from the Cromford and High Peak Railway and to Bugsworth (now called Buxworth) to receive traffic from the Peak Forest Tramway. The latter served quarries near Buxton and Doveholes. Bugsworth Basin (pictured) was a flourishing wharf with much activity around its three basins, limekilns and transhipment facilities. Today it has a forlorn atmosphere, although some restoration work is taking place.

176 At Abbeydale in the suburbs of Sheffield and close to the eastern boundary of the Peak is this steel and scythe works. It is an interesting complex of buildings and the waterwheels are regularly set in motion for visitors. The mill is easy to find alongside the A621. It dates from 1777 and work ceased in 1933. However it was re-opened during the last war to produce high quality steels.

177 The manufacture of cheese was a farmhouse occupation but it is rare to find a complete cheese press. One has been preserved at Hathersage adjacent to The George Hotel where it may be seen at the side of the main road.

178 Cheese factories were established in the late nineteenth century, especially in the south of the Peak. There were factories at Dale End near Elton, two in the Manifold Valley — at Ecton and Reapsmoor — at Hopedale near Wetton and of course at Hartington where the Stilton factory is still operational. Here is Reapsmoor factory (below) south of Longnor. It opened in the 1870s and closed in 1950, and made Derby cheeses.

179-80   This is the site of the world's very first successful water-powered cotton spinning mill. It is situated in Mill Lane, Cromford and is open to the public, having been acquired by the Arkwright Society in 1979. It was founded by Sir Richard Arkwright who lived opposite the mill. The Arkwright Society has produced a town trail which is recommended. Much of the early development of Cromford was at the hand of Arkwright and this town trail highlights his role. The earliest building is the three storey building (it was originally five storeys) behind the house.

181   The lead ore was smelted at many sites around the Peak. Many ancient sites are recorded by their name today — Bole Hill, for example. A new method of smelting was introduced in the eighteenth century which involved the reverberatory furnace. The chimney to one of these sites survives at Stone Edge on the Matlock to Chesterfield road. It dates from around 1770 and is the oldest free standing industrial chimney in Britain.

182 The working of stone has also been of much significance and the many limestone quarries which may be seen today testify to its importance. Many lime kilns exist, especially on the limestone plateau, where limestone was burnt to provide lime for the fields. Here is a good example of a single kiln which survives near Bostern Grange, above Dovedale.

183 This shows the battery of kilns at Froghall which burnt limestone from Cauldon Low Quarry before shipment by rail and canal.

184 Bradwell used to be well known for the manufacture of hard hats for miners — the Bradder Beaver, as they were known. One survived above a shippon at a farmhouse at East Ecton — a relic of the old Ecton Copper Mine, in the Manifold Valley. It was photographed together with a kibble or tub which used to be used for raising ore and rock up a mine shaft. Both are now preserved at the Peak District Mining Museum at Matlock Bath. It makes one wonder how much else survives that could have a new lease of life in our museums.

185 There are few windmills surviving around the Peak, although a new wind generator has been built to the east of Holme Bridge near Holmefirth. Mills have been restored at Heage and Dale Abbey, one survives as a dwelling at Belper and the shell of one exists on the Matlock-Chesterfield road near to Stone Edge (Fig 181). Only one seems to survive in the Peak itself — north of Hopton, close to the Hopton railway incline and it is illustrated here.

186 Sheep dipping in a nearby river was an annual occurrence and photographs survive of this happening on the River Derwent at Birchinlee and Bakewell and on the River Dove, where the stepping stones are now, near Thorpe Cloud. Another well known site was at Ashford-in-the-Water, where this bridge (pictured) is called Sheepwash Bridge. The sheep were herded into the pound in the foreground and dipped in the river at the gap in the wall on the far side of the pound.

187 This illustration shows the recently restored sheep pound adjacent to Holme Bridge at Bakewell.

188 Sheepwash at Booth Farm, Hayfield

189 Forestry plays an important part in the local economy of the moors. The Chatsworth estate also has a lot of land under timber and has a forestry exhibition at Chatsworth House. Here can be seen this stack which consists of 'ten tonnes of timber representing the amount grown every twenty four hours on 1,012 hectares of the estate woodland.'

Follies, Prospect Towers and ——Other Buildings——

The Peak is not well endowed with follies or other similar unusual buildings. Its follies are usually associated with stories of having been built to provide employment to out-of-work labourers and tend to be vantage points or belvederes to give a good view of the surrounding countryside. Some are not particularly well known, such as the prospect tower in Beresford Dale, only visible when the trees have lost their foliage. This, like its counterparts at Chatsworth and Alton Towers were private affairs, unlike Solomon's Temple at Buxton and the Victoria Tower at Matlock Bath. Other unusual buildings exist and some are well known, such as Tufa Cottage in the Via Gellia, made from the soft tufa rock, a secondary deposition of calcium carbonate. The

castle folly at Ecton is well known, probably because of its conspicuous copper spire. In contrast is The Russian Cottage on the Chatsworth Estate, a gift of the Russian Tsar. Together they make a fascinating blend of the unusual.

190   The Peak has very few follies, a few more prospect towers and a few other ornamental buildings which grace the parkland of the wealthy. This is Solomon's Temple (above) at Buxton. This photograph was taken before restoration work, which at the time of writing was being completed.

191   Boot's Folly on Bradfield Moor was built in 1927 by Mr Charles Boot to provide work for unemployed men. It can be seen across the valley from the Strines Inn. It was inspired by a similar folly on Ughill Moor.

192   This is the Victoria Prospect Tower, at the Heights of Abraham, Matlock Bath. It was built in 1844 to provide work for the unemployed. It provides a significant viewpoint down into the Derwent Valley. Today it has a 'neighbour', the cable car system from adjacent Matlock Bath railway station, which gives a view of the valley far greater than could have been contemplated by the builders of the tower!

193 The castellated top to the valve tower on Langsett Reservoir must puzzle some visitors. It is a replica of a tower at Lancaster Castle. The valves were first closed on 17 October 1904 when the reservoir began to fill.

194 Although now used as a flag tower this is known as the Hunting Tower. It is situated in the park of Chatsworth House. It is one of the few parts of the house and grounds constructed by Bess of Hardwick to have survived.

195   This tower is situated in the private grounds of the former Beresford Hall, overlooking Beresford Dale on the River Dove, south of Hartington. After the demolition of the hall in the late nineteenth century, this tower was allowed to become ruined. It was rebuilt by a Mr Green in 1905-6 using some of the mullions rescued from the remains of the hall. A vault apparently exists at the base of the tower, which stands on Castle Rock.

196   The tower in Fig 195 is a neighbour of Charles Cotton's Fishing House seen here, built in 1674, which was also in the grounds of Beresford Hall. There used to be a bowling green in front of it — although all traces of it have gone. Today it stands on private land at a bend in the Dove. It is a tangible link with the era of Cotton and Izaak Walton who used it as a base while fishing in the Dove, giving them somewhere to eat, shelter and relax. This view was taken some years ago.

197   This tower stands four square to the wind on the edge of Stanton Moor, a silhouette from the Derwent Valley up-river of Matlock. It was built in 1832 to celebrate the passing of the Reform Bill and is known as Earl Grey's Tower.

198-9   The sixth Duke of Devonshire was acquainted with Tsar Nicholas I. They had first met in 1816 when he entertained the Grand Duke Nicholas at Chatsworth. Later, in June 1826, the duke became the British Ambassador to Moscow. The duke, hoping that his friend would visit Chatsworth in 1844 during a state visit, had built the Emperor Fountain. With its 267ft-high jet of water, it was the highest in the world. A little, relatively unknown reminder of this relationship is the Russian Cottage, which Tsar Nicholas I sent to the duke in 1855. It is a copy of a model farm and built out of wood in the form of a log cabin. The gable barge boards and the window surrounds are intricately carved. The house is privately occupied and is off public rights of way. However it can be seen from the paths from Edensor and Calton Lees to Calton Houses Farm.

This picture is a close up of the barge boards.

200   This unusual private house known as 'The Hillocks', was built in 1933 and is situated at Ecton, in the Manifold Valley. It was built by Arthur Ratcliffe and replaced a single storey cottage with a thatched roof. The copper spire apparently came from a demolished chapel. The building was originally two storey and with a flat, concrete roof. The latter leaked and so another storey was added with access from a bridge from the adjacent hillside. Mr Ratcliffe was the Tory MP for Leek and was noted at the time for his lack of attendance at the House of Commons.

Archaeological Remains

The upland location of the Peak District has resulted in agriculture being predominantly pastoral rather than arable. In some areas, it is possible that some land had never been ploughed — even in prehistoric times. The absence of plough shares means that the soil has remained undisturbed. Consequently much archaeological evidence remains which has been destroyed in most other parts of Britain. In fact, the area is one of the richest areas for the archaeologist anywhere in the country. This chapter gives examples from the majority of the periods represented.

201　　This is Long Low, the longest chambered tomb in the Peak. It is situated near Damgate Farm, south of Wetton. It now has a stone wall running down its length. Bateman records its excavation in 1849 when thirteen interments were found in a cist. The ridge was 220yd in length, stretching to the south-south-west where there was another tumulus which they excavated revealing numerous burnt bones. Long Low is visible from the adjacent lane, but there is no access to the site.

202   These tall stones, the Bridestones, are the remains of a chambered burial tomb situated close to the Rushton-Congleton road on Bosley Cloud's southern flank. The two tall stones at the eastern end are over 8ft high and make this the tallest surviving single stone prehistoric monument in the Peak District.

203 There are various hillforts in the Peak District, generally ascribed to the late Bronze Age-Iron Age (ie 1000BC to the Roman invasion) although Carl Wark may be later. Carl Wark hillfort is situated north of Fox House Inn, near Longshaw where a huge defensive wall remains.

204 Another hillfort sits on top of Mam Tor at Castleton, where the circular defensive ditch remains clearly visible.

205   The only Roman fort which you can visit is at Glossop. Here the old fort, probably known as *Zerdotalia* (or *Ardotalia*) is now known as Melandra Castle. Little survives, but it is possible to view the stone foundations of the fort. It appears to have been a first century AD structure. It commanded the entrance to Longdendale — which must have been recognised as a cross Pennine route even in those days as well as the better known route over the Snake Pass, later known as Doctor's Gate.

206   Perhaps the best known archaeological feature of the district is Arbor Low, the stone circle south-west of Monyash. It is considered that the fifty-nine remaining stones were formerly vertical, although they now all lie flat. The site is an ancient monument under the protection of English Heritage. There are several stone circles in the Peak, but this is the largest and the most important site.

207   The limestone area of the Peak has many tumuli which have yielded the remains of man's early occupation of the area during the Bronze Age and Iron Age. One of the biggest tumuli is Gib Hill (above) near Arbor Low which can be easily seen on the skyline from the A515 Buxton to Ashbourne road where the Cromford and High Peak Railway crosses under the road at Parsley Hay. Both Arbor Low and Gib Hill are of the Neolithic period (3500-2000BC).

208   Another stone circle is Nine Ladies on Stanton Moor associated with the King's Stone situated nearby. It is a short distance from the Earl Grey's Tower. It is considered to belong to the Bronze Age period. It is clearly visible from a nearby footpath.

209   Here is a panoramic view of the whole of Arbor Low. It is 250ft in diameter.

210 Royston Grange Farm near to Minninglow takes its name from the medieval grange which existed here. However, excavations have revealed a Roman dwelling, fields of this period complete with stone walls and of course, remains of the medieval grange itself. The latter is shown in this picture which is on the west side of an old engine house which housed a stationary steam engine providing compressed air for drills used in a nearby quarry.

211 This illustration shows the site of the Roman dwelling. The posts indicate where post holes were located which would have supported the timber framework for the roof. The stones on the right of the illustration mark the edge of the building. An archaeological trail is obtainable from the Peak Park Joint Planning Board who now own the farm. Excavation work here still continues.

212-13 There are few buildings in the Peak which exhibit Saxon architecture. Bradbourne and Ilam seem to be the main examples where remnants can still be seen, together (possibly) with Bakewell church. Here is a doorway ascribed to the Saxon period at Ilam church, in the south wall. Inside is a very old font which could be of similar age. Both are illustrated here.

214 The only castle where substantial stone remains can still be seen is Peveril Castle at Castleton. The bailey walls date from the late eleventh or early twelfth century while the keep was erected by Henry II in 1176. Some of the thirteenth-century additions made extensive use of Roman bricks, probably from the fort at Brough. It is now in the care of English Heritage.

215 Foolow Cross was erected in its current position in 1868. It was removed from the site of the nearby chapel in 1866. The Peak is richly endowed with Saxon-medieval cross fragments many of a religious nature, whereas Wheston (opposite) and Foolow appear to have been secular.

216   Wheston Cross is a boundary cross of the medieval Royal Forest of the Peak.

Index